How to Conduct Supplier Surveys and Audits

D0556209

Janet L. Przirembel

PT Publications, Inc.
3109 45th Street
Suite 100
West Palm Beach, FL 33407-1915

Library of Congress Cataloging-in-Publication Data

Przirembel, Janet L., 1969-
    How to conduct supplier surveys and audits / Janet
    Przirembel
                p.   cm.
    Includes index.
    ISBN 0-945456-24-7 (pbk.)
    1. Industrial procurement--Auditing.   2. Purchasing--
Auditing.
    3.   Industrial surveys. I. Title.
    HD39.5.P79   1996
    657' .74--dc20   95-47471
                                                              CIP

ABOUT THE AUTHOR: Janet Przirembel is an editor with PT Publications, where she plays a vital role in preparing authors' manuscripts for publication. She is the project editor for PT Publications' series of books on Contracts Management and has also edited books on Failure Modes and Effects Analysis (FMEA), purchasing and other business topics which help companies prepare for the next century. Additionally, Ms. Przirembel was responsible for developing the *Supplier Survey and Audit Forms* software.

Prior to PT Publications, Ms. Przirembel worked in the field of Total Quality Management developing, preparing and editing technical manuals and case studies.

Ms. Przirembel holds a Bachelor of Arts Degree in English from the University of South Florida.

TABLE OF CONTENTS

PREFACE

How to Conduct Supplier Surveys and Audits addresses the crucial issues of assuring on-time delivery of 100% quantity of zero-defect material at the lowest possible cost to achieve customer satisfaction.

The first area of investigation focuses on learning the various types of surveys and learning how to use them effectively. But audits and surveys don't stop there.

In the age of World Class and Best In Class Practices, we need to develop the tools and information which are required to go beyond a survey. We need to install feedback mechanisms which accurately tell us how to measure our suppliers. The difference between old methods and new techniques of assessments can make the difference between continuous vitality and perhaps survival.

You will learn how to:

◊ develop a structural approach to surveys and audits.

◊ prepare and use the ten major criteria for evaluations.

◊ ensure that customer requirements are continuously met.

◊ determine team members and define their roles in the process.

◊ develop techniques for evaluating a supplier.

◊ prepare a survey which covers the process and systems.

How to Use this Book

This book is designed to be used in conjunction with the corollary texts in our Purchasing Series. Please call us at the number below for more information about utilizing our tools. The idea behind this book is to read it with a pen in your hand so that you can answer the questions and write down the plans you are going to put into action. For those people who use this book alone, there is enough information to get you started on the road to excellence. Remember, however, that roadmaps such as this book are best accompanied by travel guides such as the ones we offer in the field of purchasing. Together, they can make your journey a rewarding one.

HELP DESK HOTLINE

1-800-272-4335

In order to answer the questions of our readers, we have established a Help Desk Hotline at our corporate headquarters in West Palm Beach, Florida. We invite you to call us with your queries about how to use the forms and tools in this book.

We also invite you to use our HELP DESK HOTLINE to find out more about other books we publish, as well as our *Supplier Surveys and Audits Forms* software and a videotape series entitled **Supplier Certification: The Path to Excellence**. In addition to books, software and videotapes, we offer over 80 courses which can be scheduled for intensive, in-house seminars. Call us for details.

SUPPLIER
AUDIT
PLANNING

CHAPTER ONE

Definitions

Survey: To examine and determine with qualified data, the supplier's potential and ability to conform to customer requirements.

Audit: The evaluation process on a continuous and random basis to determine adherence to customer requirements.

What are the major considerations for conducting a survey and audit?

The business strategic plan requires goals that are set and achieved:

◊   Zero defects or Six Sigma performance

◊   Commitment to customer service

◊   Total management commitment

◊   Reduction of inventory and increased inventory turns

◊   Supplier/customer satisfaction

◊   100% quality, quantity, delivery

A well organized business strategic plan provides direction to the entire corporation. It spells out their function and inspires every department to focus on the overall goal. It:

◊   is developed by management.

◊   provides a clear vision for the future.

The goals start with **QUALITY AT THE SOURCE:**

◊   Six Sigma

◊   Customer service

◊   Education/training

◊   Statistical Process Control

◊   Total Quality Management

◊   Supplier Certification

◊   Responsiveness to change

◊   Monitoring progress (self)

◊   Setting specific objectives

◊   Internal/external satisfaction

◊   Employee involvement/empowerment

The Supplier Selection Team

Teams have been proven to be effective in problem analysis and solution. They must be managed properly, and there must be pressure for results. This result-orientation will ensure that progress will be made, but  should not result in fear or unnecessary stress.

Who should be represented on a survey team? What functions? What levels? The first step in selecting partners is not to designate one function as solely responsible for selection. You will have difficulty entering into a partnership with a supplier if you haven't established a partnership between the existing functions within your company.

Organization Structure

◊ Function representation

◊ Select a leader

◊ Buy-in process

◊ Ownership/responsibility

◊ Cross-functional team

Other considerations to include in a company structure to perform an audit and survey efficiently are:

◊ Engineering requirements

◊ Quality requirements

◊ Customer requirements

The supplier selection team should be composed of representatives from at least the following departments.

◊ Engineering – design, manufacturing, industrial, etc.

◊ Manufacturing – operations, process

◊ Supply Management – international, domestic, commodity

◊ Finance – cost accounting

◊ Quality – supplier quality engineer, manager

Qualifications of Team Members

◊ Knowledge of the supplier process

◊ Experienced both in requirements and the audit/survey process

◊ Professional approval and attitude

◊ Practical/pragmatic

◊ Analytical "mind-set" approach

What are the critical factors/concerns in examining/evaluating a supplier?

☑ _____

_____

_____

_____

_____

_____

_____

Tracking

Before partnering with a supplier, you'll want to determine if a supplier is in good enough shape to work in a symbiotic relationship with your company. Existing data on present suppliers should be organized and used by the survey team and should include, but not be limited to, the following:

◊ Incoming quality history

◊ Past performance

◊ On-time delivery

◊ Quality discrepancy

◊ First article inspection

◊ Line feedback

◊ Warranty failures

Note: If you are dealing with a new supplier, you should utilize their data. If incomplete or nonexistent, think twice about that supplier. Otherwise, you will end up constantly expediting performance improvement, becoming their Mommy or Daddy!!

Listed below are the reasons for tracking suppliers.

◊ Proactive vs. reactive

◊ Avoidance of problems

◊ Obtaining insight

◊ Providing measurement

◊ Opportunity for redirection

Required resources include:

◊   people.

◊   facilities.

◊   equipment.

◊   money.

When surveying a supplier, you'll want to examine the following areas ...

◊   Quality   ◊   Warehouse

◊   Management   ◊   Other options

◊   Systems   ◊   Receiving

◊   Purchasing   ◊   Shipping

◊   Engineering   ◊   Maintenance

◊   Finance/Accounting   ◊   Inventory control

◊   Sales/Marketing   ◊   Direct labor

◊   Research & Development

◊   Direct labor

... and take into account the considerations listed on the following page. On page 37 in Chapter 5, we share with you a survey form that lists 14 major areas to consider in designing your survey.

Major Considerations	Development Considerations	Minor Considerations
• Management commitment • Quality SPC/TQC • Delivery • Quantity • Total cost	• Design capability • Flexibility in manufacturing • Lot control • Location • Service • Design for producibility	• Written procedures • Location • Material control • Union vs. Nonunion • Personality • Housekeeping • Workers' attitudes • Control

Different Types of Sources:

◊ **Multiple** – When a company decides to utilize more than one source for the same item or commodity purchased.

◊ **Single** – A single-source supplier that you choose to buy from, although other suppliers exist. With a single source supplier you have the option when demand increases to turn to other suppliers to meet your needs.

◊ **Sole** – A sole-source supplier is one that is unique; literally the only source for a needed part.

What are the issues to be considered with each?

☑ _____

_____

_____

_____

_____

As a result of the Industrial Revolution, there came the need for standardization of components. Then the need for consistency of quality evolved very quickly.

We then developed methods for improving quality through control.

Inspection + Detection = Part Control

Led to Acceptable Quality Levels (AQL) or A Quick Look

As we now find ourselves in a World Market, we recognize these past methods are outdated.

Today's leaders are implementing Six Sigma programs and Statistical Process Control (SPC). But it's not enough that we only apply SPC to our facilities. We need to:

 **INVOLVE THE SUPPLIER BASE AS WELL! EARLY INVOLVEMENT!**

SUPPLIER POSITIONING

CHAPTER TWO

The next step is selecting the suppliers to be surveyed and developed. We suggest utilizing our matrix and grid determine which suppliers to survey. One thing is certain: we do not have the resources of money, people, or time to survey all suppliers. Our intent is to develop a strategic plan and direction for surveys.

Supplier Objectives

◊   What is the critical first step?

◊   Reduce the number of suppliers

◊   How many is enough?

◊   Supplier development

◊   Long-term agreements

◊   Consistent improvements

Market Elements

Prioritize the elements of selection based on your type of business.

◊ Established, mature market

◊ Moderate changes in market demands

◊ High-tech, fast changing

Key Strategic Steps

◊ Low number of suppliers

◊ Supplier Certification

◊ Objective/performance data

◊ Long-term business commitment

◊ Common interest

◊ Consistent quality standards

◊ Geographic location

◊ Management commitment

Supplier Positioning Matrix

This process requires a different method of working with suppliers. You need to:

◊ achieve early supplier involvement

◊ have common vision.

◊ have trust in the relationship.

◊ communicate frequently.

Supplier Positioning Matrix

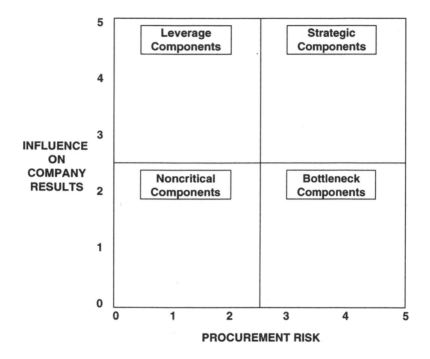

First you'll need to position your existing supplier base and then place them in an order which distinguishes good and bad performers. When reviewing the supplier base to determine a reasonable number that we can work with in an efficient and productive manner, we can apply Pareto's law to the existing supplier base. Pareto's law says that 20% of your suppliers account for 80% of your procurement costs.

This grid shows the two important factors to consider when selecting a supplier: influence on company results and procurement risk. For each supplier, you'll need to determine the market success elements, weight those elements relative to market success, then calculate the overall influence. Then you'll need to calculate the procurement risk for the supplier by determining the relative strength of the competitive forces:

◊ bargaining power.

◊ rivalry.

◊ substitution.

◊ entry barriers.

The number of suppliers is important, but the four types of suppliers needs to be looked at as well.

◊ Strategic Supplier

- Delivers a product/service essential to your business

- A closer relationship makes an important contribution to your competitiveness and gives advantages to the supplier

◊ Leverage Supplier

- One of a wide range of suppliers in the market

- Provides a product/service essential to your business

- Closer relationship has no value

◊ Noncritical Supplier

- Provides a low value product/service not essential to your business

- Many alternate suppliers

◊ Bottleneck Supplier

- Sole supplier for product/service
- Controls market
- Establishes price

An example of how the required number of suppliers may be distributed between the four types of suppliers is shown on the following page.

TOTAL QUALITY CONTROL RECOG-NIZES THAT EVERYONE IS RESPONSIBLE FOR THE QUALITY OF HIS OR HER WORK.

Commodity	Present Number of Suppliers	Required Number of Suppliers	Strategic Suppliers	Leverage Suppliers	Noncritical Suppliers	Bottleneck Suppliers
CRT's	2	2	1	1	0	0
Printheads	3	3	0	3	0	0
Elec. Dist.	35	5	0	0	5	0
Machine Shop	18	3	0	0	3	0
Motors	7	4	0	4	0	0
Power Supply	5	4	1	3	0	0
Rollers	4	2	0	0	2	0
Assembly	8	3	0	3	0	0
PCB's	9	2	1	1	0	0
Keypads / boards	3	3	1	2	0	0
Sheet Metal	9	3	0	3	0	0
Gears	2	2	2	0	0	0
Hardware	20	10	1	0	8	1
Springs	6	2	0	0	2	0
Magnetics	2	2	0	0	2	0
Glass	2	2	0	0	2	0
Extrusion	1	1	1	0	0	0
Vacuum Injection	10	7	0	7	0	0
Packing Material	2	1	1	0	0	0
Bearings	1	1	1	0	0	0
Labels / Logos	5	2	0	0	2	0
Plastics	4	1	1	0	0	0
Cable / Wire	4	2	0	2	0	0
Magnets	1	1	0	0	1	0
Solenoid / Clutch	2	2	0	0	2	0
Ribbons	1	2	0	2	0	0
Locks	2	2	0	2	0	0
Dust Covers	1	1	0	1	0	0
Power Cords	1	1	0	1	0	0
Batteries	1	1	0	1	0	0
Keycaps	1	1	0	1	0	0
TOTALS	172	78	11	37	29	1

HUMAN RESOURCES REQUIRED

CHAPTER THREE

Qualifications of surveyors or auditors should include as a minimum the skills required to perform an excellent job. Remember, suppliers become victims when an auditor is hostile. Some other qualifications and factors include:

◊ Analytical/quantitative

◊ Excellent interpersonal skills

◊ Technical competence (specific to the supplier's process whenever possible)

◊ Commitment and professionalism

◊ Ethics

◊ Lead auditor training

◊ Team training

The survey must be planned and systematic, using some form of working papers to ensure that all facets are covered and quantified (both comprehensive coverage and administration).

Some Techniques to Use When Conducting a Survey:

◊ Put the person at ease with:
- a simple introduction.
- a discussion topic other than business.
- a review of the agenda.

◊ Explain your purpose and include:
- the objectives of the day.
- why you're asking questions.

◊ Display competence – dress accordingly.

◊ Don't discuss what you have seen elsewhere ("show off").

◊ Analyze the response.
- Think out loud – playback.
- Deter variance responses.

◊ Give tentative conclusion.
- No secrets.
- Overview positives, negatives.
- Allow for clarification.

◊ Explain the next step.
- Need more information?
- How did they do in the interview?

Some Techniques to Use For Validation of Findings:

◊ Follow survey/audit questions.

◊ Follow incomplete responses with, "And then what happens?"

◊ Have them "show and tell."

◊ Use concrete, visual examples.

When Conducting a Survey, Auditor Objectives Include:

◊ Be a good listener.

◊ Notice regulations.

◊ Ask positive questions.

◊ Check competency level.

◊ Don't throw stones.

◊ Be helpful.

◊ Look for high morale.

◊ Results-oriented approach.

◊ Be confident/authoritative.

◊ Be confidential.

◊ Understand cultures.

When Analyzing Results:

◊ Complete scoring each date.

◊ Review comments.

◊ Complete form within 48 hours.

◊ Write comments down.

◊ Write letter of findings and scores.

◊ Meet with suppliers.

◊ Identify corrections, action and timetable.

◊ Receive supplier's answers.

◊ Identify other suppliers to survey new source.

◊ Benchmark suppliers on form.

◊ Meet minimum requirement timetable.

The Win/Win Philosophy

The survey must reinforce the supplier's strong points and strengths while identifying their shortcomings and weaknesses.

Objective performance data is preferable to subjective data, whenever possible. When data is subjective, more than one person must rate the supplier.

 BE FAIR, NOT EASY!

Surveyor/Auditor Basic Education Training and Requirements

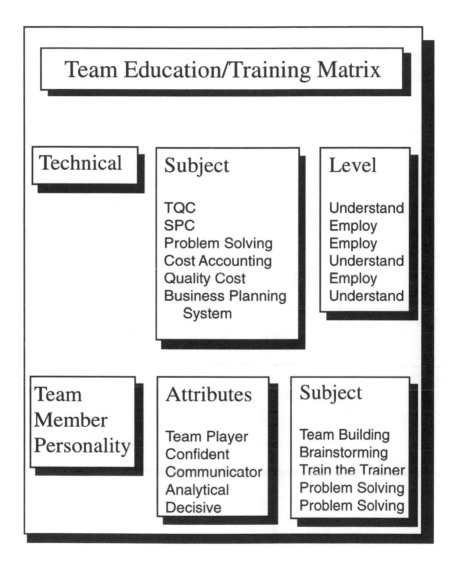

Team Education/Training Matrix

Technical

Subject	Level
TQC	Understand
SPC	Employ
Problem Solving	Employ
Cost Accounting	Understand
Quality Cost	Employ
Business Planning System	Understand

Team Member Personality

Attributes	Subject
Team Player	Team Building
Confident	Brainstorming
Communicator	Train the Trainer
Analytical	Problem Solving
Decisive	Problem Solving

Team Leader Role

The matrix on the previous page gives you an idea of the attributes and requirements which are necessary for members of the survey and audit team. But the team leader is also a vital part of the team, guiding the group throughout the entire survey and audit process from start to finish and ensuring the activities are kept on schedule. Each organization will have different requirements for its team leaders. However, there are two requirements essential to all team leaders. They must be:

◊   experienced in the surveys and audits process.

◊   completely familiar with all elements and guidelines in the surveys and audits process.

Management Maturity Levels

The first indicators of a supplier's potential to be certified are company-wide in nature – management commitment and organizational status. These elements, of course, can also be used to determine your own management maturity levels. Let's look first at the levels of understanding and attitude.

At the first level, a company's management has no comprehension whatsoever of Supplier Certification, Just-in-Time, or Total Quality Management. At the second level, management is aware of what must be done, but have committed no dollars to the program. As money is added, management rises to the third level in which they are willing to learn and support expansion of Supplier Certification programs.

At the fourth level, management is actively participating in quality and manufacturing control programs. The suppliers of level four companies are actively involved with quality in this process. The fifth level is the goal that both customers and suppliers want to attain. At this level, management sees Supplier Certification as an integral part of their company.

Both the status of the company as a whole and the status of the quality of its organization go hand-in-hand with management maturity levels. The chart on the next page shows the characteristics of a company at each of the five levels.

You should be looking for suppliers who rank in Level 3 to Level 5 on all three scales. There is some measure of management commitment at this level, which is essential to the success of a Supplier Certification program.

Levels	Management Traits	Quality Organization	Company Status
1	Lack of understanding	No inspector present	Unaware of what causes poor quality
2	Sees value of change, but no commitment of money	Firefighting mode; Symptoms treated, not causes	Constant quality problems are present
3	Willing to change, support, and learn	Management becomes involved in prevention	Commitment to continuous improvement
4	Management is participating	Quality effectively controls process	Shift to defect prevention
5	Management is part of improvement team	Zero-defects is the only acceptable method	Supplier Certification is a way of life

Human Resources Chapter Two

REPORTING: THE PATH TOWARD IMPROVEMENT

CHAPTER FOUR

The process of a survey and audit is to have a CIP method in place that works effectively.

◊ Findings
  • Statement of fact
  • Noncompliance
  • Supported by evidence

◊ Observations
  • Detect weakness
  • Result in degradation
  • Results

◊ Briefing
  • Short, frequent meetings
  • Compile data and ranking

- Summarizing and prioritizing
- Synopsis
◊ Presentation

Survey Summary

Areas to be noted:

◊ Cleanliness of the facility in all areas from production to laboratories and breakrooms. Appropriate cleanliness is a must for the production of quality. Good Manufacturing Practices (GMP) are recommended.

◊ A quality assurance function to interrelate separate departments and to assist nontechnical employees in comprehending their positions' quality requirements.

◊ A testing or calibration laboratory operating in total quality control.

◊ A system for review, documentation, and control of changes to specifications for raw materials and products, procedures, test methods, and storage conditions.

◊ Review process control systems.

◊ Testing and inspection programs which apply the most current knowledge of chemistry, statistics, and the production process.

◊ Adequate storage system.

◊ An evaluation of the commitment of the personnel to quality.

◊ A training program to assure the knowledge needed to perform a given job.

◊ A lot traceability system.

◊ Survey program existence, format, and schedule.

◊ Producibility of product.

◊ Review the survey summary with the Program Coordinator.

◊ Write up post-survey summary to the supplier – one paragraph per summary section. This should be completed one week after survey has been performed.

◊ Review the post-survey summary letter with the Program Coordinator prior to mailing to the supplier.

Continuous Improvement Process

◊ Frequent meetings

◊ Written agendas

◊ Written findings

◊ Demonstrated results

◊ The survey report and details are prepared by the audit team.

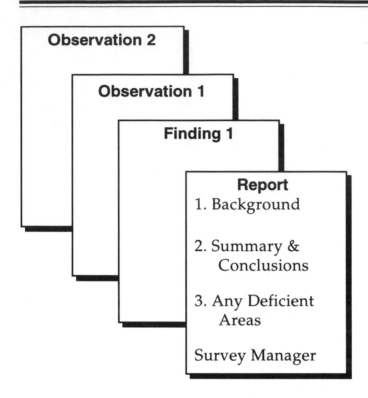

The client (Survey Manager) reviews the package and then attaches a cover letter containing the information shown on the next page.

```
Date:
  To:
From:
Subject: Survey of ...

Brief Background

Executive Summary
of Results

Requests for
Corrective Action
```

Or the survey team may decide that the process of Supplier Certification should be the responsibility of the Buyer/Planner or team member. This process may begin with a memo which is sent by the initiator who is recommending the candidate to the Supplier Certification Steering Committee. This memo should include the following information on the supplier:

◊ Name and code

◊ Street address with city, state and zip code

◊ Phone number

◊ Contact person and his/her title

◊ Number of open purchase orders

◊ Number of part numbers

◊ Yearly volume in dollars

◊ Present delivery rating

◊ Present quality rating

◊   Primary commodities provided by supplier

◊   What long-term contracts have been awarded to the supplier

Post-Survey Activity

Once a survey has been conducted and evaluated, the next job is to write a final report which recommends whether or not a supplier is capable of being first qualified and then certified. The post-survey summary form should capture the following information:

◊   Company name, address (including city, state, and zip code), and phone number

◊   Contact

◊   Supplier code

◊   Name of surveyor

◊   Who accompanied the supplier

◊   Initial survey date, survey date, and audit date

◊   Supplier score

◊   Minimum score required

◊   Recommendations

◊   Date when action plan is due

◊   Place for supplier's acknowledgment

An example of a post-survey summary form can be found in Chapter Four of *Supplier Certification II: A Handbook for Achieving Excellence Through Continuous Improvement* (PT Publications; West Palm Beach, FL).

A copy of the completed survey with the final report should be sent to the supplier, whatever the recommendation. We have seen many instances of suppliers who have taken areas of weakness and turned them into positive programs of improvement. Many of these suppliers have eventually gone on to become certified. In a certain sense, the final report is free consulting. Companies that want to improve their performance will use it to their advantage. Companies who ignore it will most likely become extinct.

As for the recommendation, there are three categories. Each requires a different set of post-survey activities. Refer to *Supplier Certification II: A Handbook for Achieving Excellence Through Continuous Improvement* (PT Publications; West Palm Beach, FL) for examples of the documentation discussed in each category.

1. Not Recommended

The supplier in this case has no evidence or documentation of a control system; major defects in the control system; or, cannot demonstrate an acceptable process. The deficiency in the control system/process will require in excess of 60 days to correct.

A "Supplier Corrective Action" report will be issued requesting correction of these discrepancies. Upon receipt of satisfactory answers, a resurvey will be required. At that time the supplier may be moved to conditional status.

You can use a letter to notify suppliers who were not recommended for entry into the company's Supplier Certification Program. This letter should include the date of the survey, the names of your company representatives present, and the supplier representatives present. It should clearly state the supplier's company has *not been recommended* to enter in to the Supplier Certification Process due to the findings recorded during the evaluation survey.

2. Conditionally Recommended to the QSL List

The supplier has inadequacies in its control system documentation, but the process appears to be working satisfactorily. A "Supplier Corrective Action" report will be issued requesting the supplier to submit an improvement plan for each of the discrepancies. If the plan is not submitted within 60 days, the rating will be changed to "Not Recommended." For suppliers in this category, you should sign a conditional agreement with the supplier where the supplier states that the discrepancy and/or deficiencies described in the report are verified and will be corrected by the date designated in the action plan. It should also note that the supplier status will be upgraded to "recommended" when purchasing receives written evidence of the promised corrective action on or before the agreed dates and determines that it meets the survey's minimum requirements.

3. Recommended to the QSL List

The supplier has adequate document evidence of compliance and meets the minimum point value. In addition, the supplier's demonstrated process appears to be working satisfactorily. Within this category are suppliers who are ready and willing to undergo the certification process. The next step is to develop a supplier partnership.

Your acceptance letter should congratulate the supplier for successfully achieving the status of "QUALIFIED SUPPLIER." You should also let them know your Supplier Certification team will be contacting them to start the first phase in the implementation of the certification program. You may want to conclude your letter by thanking them for their efforts in meeting this milestone and for their continued participation in the process.

SUPPLIER AUDITS AND SURVEYS

CHAPTER FIVE

If the first part of the Supplier Certification journey is learning the Total Quality Management (TQM) mind-set and preparing a list of supplier selection criteria, then the second part is surveying suppliers to determine whether they meet a quantitated level of acceptance.

In general, the criteria looks for two things—the presence of a sound total business process and a manufacturing process which is under control.

One of the more frequent questions asked is: "What is the difference between a supplier survey and a supplier audit?" In its simplest terms, a survey of a supplier is conducted before it manufactures a product. The survey determines what is happening at the supplier's plant. An audit, on the other hand, is conducted after a supplier be-

---

gins making a product. Its purpose is to assure us that what we want to happen is, indeed, happening at the supplier's plant. A survey is used to find a supplier capable of producing zero-defect parts which will be shipped on time. An audit can be thought of as a maintenance tool, whereby we check to see that the supplier's quality and manufacturing process remain under control. An audit can also be used as a method to improve a supplier's performance by pointing out weaknesses. It can point out areas where more education and training is needed. (See Tape Four in our Video Education Series, "Supplier Certification: The Path to Excellence.")

The following flow chart shows the sequence of actions in implementing a supplier survey.

SUPPLIER QUALIFICATION
FLOW CHART

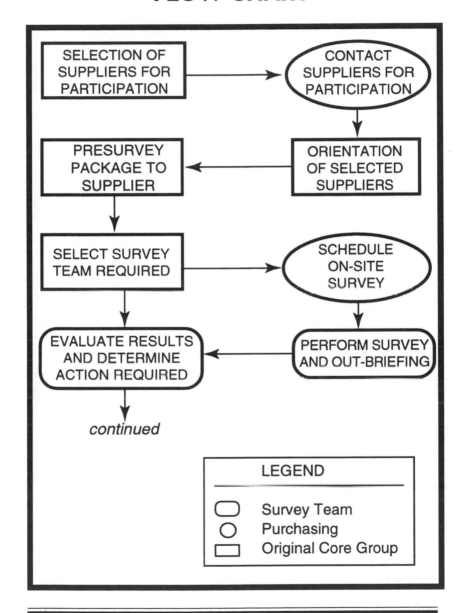

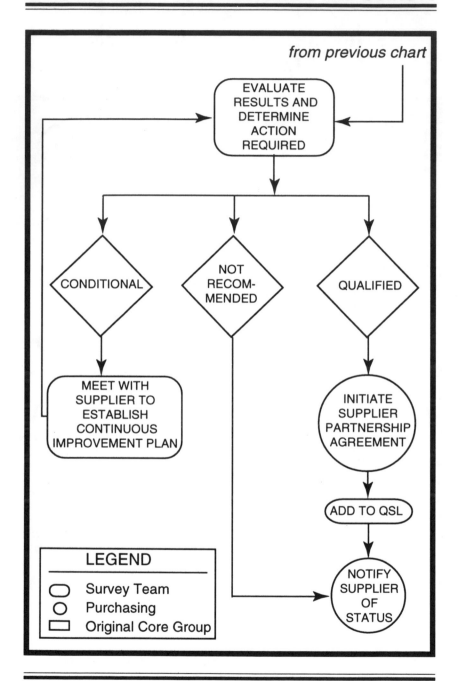

from previous chart

EVALUATE RESULTS AND DETERMINE ACTION REQUIRED

CONDITIONAL

NOT RECOM- MENDED

QUALIFIED

MEET WITH SUPPLIER TO ESTABLISH CONTINUOUS IMPROVEMENT PLAN

INITIATE SUPPLIER PARTNERSHIP AGREEMENT

ADD TO QSL

NOTIFY SUPPLIER OF STATUS

LEGEND

⬭ Survey Team
◯ Purchasing
▭ Original Core Group

Forms of Survey	Types of Survey
• ISO 9000 • Malcolm Baldrige • External Consultant • Motorola QSR • European Quality Award • Customer Surveys	• Distributors • Software Suppliers • Maintenance, Repair, and Ordering • Original Manufacturers • Equipment Suppliers • Professional Services

Supplier Qualification Process Evaluation

◊ Management commitment

◊ Finances/total cost control

◊ Manufacturing control

◊ Capability and capacity

◊ Facilities and equipment

◊ Statistical Process Control

◊ Tool and gage maintenance

◊ Sub-tier suppliers (procurement)

◊ Internal measurements of suppliers

◊ Configuration

◊ Research and Development

◊ Quality management and information

◊ Materials Management

Evaluating Suppliers

Evaluating suppliers must be quantified with no subjectivity entering into the evaluation. You do this by assigning a point value to each criterion. That is what companies do when they use a Supplier Certification program to determine which suppliers are World Class and which ones will not be able to make the grade. Surveys and audits using quantifiable questions are of extreme importance. Do not take a short cut for this step.

DON'T ASK: Do I feel like this supplier can make the product?

ASK: Does the supplier have his plant processes under control and the capability to make the product?

The first question elicits fuzzy answers. The answers to the second question can be objectively quantified, using the point values listed on the next page as we record responses and gather evidence for the selection criteria.

Based on the point values, suppliers are divided into six rating categories. Those who fall into the **Poor** and **Weak** categories are not suppliers you would want to make a commitment to work with. They do not meet even the most minimal quality requirements. A **Fair** rating represents a marginal supplier who may have the potential to become approved within a reasonable amount of time. An **Approved** supplier meets the minimum requirements you have established for doing business with your company. A **Qualified** supplier has a commitment to quality and is a sound potential candidate for Supplier Certification. An **Excellent** supplier is one of the most difficult to find, even worldwide. But an **Excellent** rating is the ultimate goal!

Evaluation Criteria Point Value

Question Score Points		Approach	Deployment	Results
0	Poor	• No system evident • No management recognition evident	• None	• Anecdotal
2	Weak	• Beginnings of system/process • Limited resource commitment	• Some activities started • Deployment in some areas	• Some evidence of output • Limited results
4	Fair	• Prevention-based system defined • Less than total mgmt. support	• Deployed in some major areas and some support areas	• Inconsistent, but positive results
6	Approved	• Sound system in place with evidence of evaluation/ improvement cycles • Some evidence of business integration • Proactive leadership emerging	• Deployed in most major areas and some support areas • Mostly consistent and accepted	• Positive trends in most areas • Evidence that results caused by approach
8	Qualified	• Well-designed system/process with evidence of Continuous Improvement Program • Good to excellent integration • Total mgmt. support	• Consistent across all major areas and most support areas • Consistent and pervasively accepted	• Positive trends and demonstrated results • All require-ments met
10	Excellent	• Systematic preven-tion that anticipates customer needs • Total management leadership and commitment • Publicly acknowl-edged and industry recognized	• Consistent across all major areas and support areas • All operations	• Excellent, sustained results • Exceeds requirements • World Class

The following statement of purpose was developed by a client in starting their survey process.

"To survey a supplier's manufacturing environment in a way that examines and evaluates objective evidence, that applicable elements of the quality assurance, operations and materials programs have been developed, documented and effectively implemented in accordance with specified requirements so that the supplier can be considered for supplier certification."

We recommend that a Presurvey Questionnaire be sent out before you conduct a supplier survey. This presurvey is for informational purposes only and not all the questions are applicable to all the companies that are asked to fill it out. Besides company ownership, financial information and type of business, the questionnaire attempts to ascertain how sophisticated the supplier's current quality practices are and whether the supplier is moving toward Statistical Process Control (SPC) and Total Quality Management (TQM).

Its purpose is also to find out if the supplier is already certified by another company. If it is, then the certification process will go much faster for a pre-certified supplier. In addition, this tool reduces the number of suppliers down to a more manageable level: just those with whom you should conduct a survey. You simply cannot survey all suppliers in every commodity. Use this tool to identify the best.

PRESURVEY QUESTIONNAIRE

The purpose of this questionnaire is to get acquainted with various aspects of the supplier's company. We need the information to evaluate their organization. Suppliers will also need to be provided with complete assurance that this questionnaire is strictly confidential. The contents will only be used internally and exclusively for the evaluation of the supplier's readiness in our "ACHIEVING EXCELLENCE THROUGH CONTINUOUS IMPROVEMENT" program.

INSTRUCTIONS: All of the following questions should be answered by the supplier. Any questions that do not pertain to the supplier's business operations should be identified as not applicable (N/A). If the answer to a particular question is "none," please write that down. We regret that we will be unable to process incomplete questionnaires. Attach additional sheets when necessary to address specific questions.

PRESURVEY

GENERAL INFORMATION:

Company Name Five Star Manufacturing
Company SIC 0312

Mailing Address_____PO Box 1403_____

_____Marshville, IL 39407-1917_____

_____

Telephone Number (407) 257-8699
Fax Number (407) 257-8010

STATUS OF OWNERSHIP:

  ___ Proprietorship ___ Division
  ___ Partnership _12_ Years in business
  _X_ Corporation ___ Public
  ___ Subsidiary ___ Private
  ___ Affiliate

Parent Company (if applicable)

Has your company done business with us
in the past? _X_ Yes ___ No
If yes, when? ____1996____

BUSINESS STATUS:

___ Small   ___ Large
___ Minority Owned   X Medium
___ Woman Owned   ___ Foreign
___ Handicapped (not for profit)

TYPE OF BUSINESS:

 X Manufacturing   ___ Raw Material
___ Service   X Assembly
___ Distributor

FACILITIES:

Plant Size 400,000 Sq. Ft.
Plant Condition Good
Equipment Condition Good
Number of Production Shifts ____
Total Number of Employees ____
200 Production   15 Engineering
 5 Service   ___ R&D
30 Administration   9 Sales & Marketing

List all your facilities by location _____

_____

_____

CONTACTS:

	Contact Person	Telephone
Sales	James Duhon	252-8744
Quality	Thomas Duvall	252-8703
Purchasing	Frank King	252-8760
Delivery	Sarah Silver	252-8306
Production Control	William Frank	252-8740
General Manager	Barry Larkow	257-8700

LISTING OF KEY PERSONNEL:

President & CEO	Robert Presnor
Vice President - Operations	Barry Larkow
Vice President - Finance	Stephan Rogers
Vice President - Marketing	James Duhon
Vice President - Engineering	Harry Carson
Production Manager	Louis Lumpur
Quality Manager	Thomas Duvall
Customer Services Manager	Barbara Condike

PAYMENT AND DELIVERY TERMS:

Normal payment terms __Net 30 Days__

Normal FOB point _____

FINANCIAL INFORMATION:

D&B rating ___A+___

    Taxpayer identification number   _UV 437-9742-030_

    Financial statements provided for year(s)
    _1994_ (attached) _1996_

    Annual sales revenues for last three years:

(YEAR)	(SALES REVENUES)
1994	29,000,000
1995	30,000,000
1996	32,000,000

Do you currently track cost of quality? _X_ Yes ___ No

Are your records available for audit? _X_ Yes ___ No

What are your annual shipments (average 2 years)?
  See Attached

What percentage of your annual shipments are
                 procured by our company? _20_ %

What is your total past due committed
                 shipments (in dollars)? _____

Credit references we can contact:

(COMPANY)	(ADDRESS)	(TELEPHONE)
National Bank	High Street (Cromell)	629-4037
Vista Corporation	Marsh Road (Cromell)	536-3200
Max Credit	Lipton Road	629-4799
US General	Semist Street	629-8625
Citibank	Lipton Road	539-3600

PRODUCTS AND VOLUMES:
Products produced

Machined Parts, Subassemblies, Special Equipment

Services performed

Design/Build Special Equipment

Volumes produced (Lot Size)

X Low   ___ Medium   ___ High

ENGINEERING CAPABILITIES:

Desirable engineering services your company offers

Design, Build, Test, Install

ADDITIONAL COMMENTS:
Very broad-based, enabling total business support

QUALITY MANAGEMENT: Yes   No

Are you a certified supplier for any
other customer?   X   ___
If yes, who?   Barkin Products

QUALITY MANAGEMENT CONT.

	Yes	No
Are you ISO 9000 registered?	___	X

If yes, under what category?

___ (9001)	___ (9003)
___ (9002)	___ (9004)

	Yes	No
Have you committed the organization to TQM?	X	___

What type of quality system do you employ?
 ISO Format

	Yes	No
Do you routinely provide certifications with your shipments of products?	X	___
Do you have a written Quality Manual?	X	___
Do you use a formal supplier certification process in your procurement activities?	___	___

Do you routinely track customer service levels for:

 X On-time delivery?
 X Quality?
 X Count accuracy?

What type of material control system do you have? Material Traceability

PROCESS CONTROL:

Record the elements that apply to the process control system used in your company:

	Yes	No
Statistical Process Control	X	___
Process Routing	X	___
Routing ID by Customer Number	___	X
Tooling Controlled	X	___
Special Handling	X	___
In-Process Revision System	___	X
Time Standards Used	X	___

LIST OF EQUIPMENT USED IN PRODUCTS SOLD OR SERVICES PROVIDED TO OUR COMPANY:

1993	VTL CNC	1995	CNCCMM
1992	Lath CNC	1950	Remanufactured Grinder
1995	Horizontal CNC		
1995	Movarch		

ATTACHMENTS:

Please attach any documents you feel will assist us in evaluating your organization.

THE INFORMATION CONTAINED HEREIN IS COMPLETE AND ACCURATE TO THE BEST OF MY KNOWLEDGE AND BELIEF.

Robert Presnor   President & CEO

Signature of Authorized Representative   **Title**

Robert Presnor

Print Name

Five Star Manufacturing   9/9/96

Company Name   **Date**

PLEASE RETURN TO THE ATTENTION OF:

DOCUMENTS REQUIRED WITH PRESURVEY:

> Annual Survey
> Quality Policy and Manual
> Company Brochures and Literature
> Facility Listing — Equipment and Process
>
> Annual Reports
>
> Financial Statements

FOR INTERNAL USE ONLY: DATE: 9/11/96

Comments

Reviewed by *Robert Parrish*

Chapter One listed a number of areas and considerations you can take into account when surveying suppliers. These criteria need to be put into a survey format which will allow you to gather the information necessary for successful supply management. The remainder of this chapter provides you with an example of a completed survey. However, many companies use more than one survey. For additional surveys, please consult the *Supply Management Toolbox* (PT Publications, Inc.; West Palm Beach, FL).

The following general survey has several parts: the Survey Scoring Summary (which weights each category of the survey), 14 sections each covering an individual area (such as Total Quality Management, Documentation and Record Control, and Process Control, and the Summary Sheet) which shows how the supplier scored on each question in each section of each section of the survey.

GENERAL SURVEY & AUDIT FORM

Date _9/10/96_

Supplier Company	Five Star Manufacturing	
Address	PO Box 1403	
	Marshville, IL 39407-1917	
Survey Contact Person	**Name** Frank King	
	Phone 407-252-8760	
	Fax 407-257-8010	
Survey/Audit Team	**Supply Leader** Jennifer McCormick	Purchasing
	Chris Jones	Quality
	Scott Keller	Engineering

Survey Scoring Summary

Selection Category	Total Points Avail.	Points Awd.	Weight Factor	Score
1 Total Quality Management	100	83	.10	8.3
2 Total Cost	100	77	.08	6.2
3 Material Control	100	79	.10	7.9
4 Process Control	100	80	.10	8.0
5 Safety and Housekeeping	100	83	.05	4.1
6 Documentation and Record Control	100	77	.05	3.8
7 Organization and Administration	100	87	.05	4.3
8 Customer Service and Satisfaction	100	88	.08	7.0
9 Information Management	100	88	.06	5.3
10 Supply Management	100	71	.08	5.7
11 Design and Product Development	100	63	.07	4.4
12 Capacity	100	86	.05	4.3
13 Delivery and Shipping	100	85	.08	6.8
14 GMP, Labor Relations, and Regulatory Compliance	100	89	.05	4.4
Total	**1400**		**1.00**	

Total Score 80.5

CATEGORY 1: Total Quality Management

		YES	NO	POINTS
1.	Does the supplier use a formal quality system?	X	—	4
2.	Is there a written corporate quality policy?	X	—	5
3.	Does the supplier have a QA manual? ✔ Supplied 6 mo. Latest Revision	X	—	5
4.	Are all levels of the plant trained in Total Quality Management?	X	—	4
5.	Is precision measuring equipment calibrated and records well maintained?	X	—	5
6.	Are records of inspection and process control accurate and current?	X	—	3
7.	Is there a segregated QC lab or inspection area?	—	X	4 N/A Lab
8.	Is quality data used as a basis for corrective action?	X	—	3
9.	Does the operator have the authority to stop the production line if there is a quality problem?	X	—	4
10.	Is supplier's quality system based upon statistical methodologies?	X	—	4
11.	Does supplier's quality system have a written procedure for corrective action when a defect occurs?	X	—	4
12.	Does the supplier have a system of internal surveys and audits to ensure the proper functioning of its quality system?	X	—	4
13.	Does the supplier's organizational structure support the customer's quality requirements?	X	—	5
14.	Does the supplier support operator control versus product inspection?	X	—	4
15.	Are meetings of quality teams held regularly?	X	—	5
16.	Is achieving World Class status part of the supplier's quality improvement plans?	X	—	3

		YES	NO	POINTS
17.	Is the supplier's quality system certified by another customer? Who? Capwell Bros.	X	__	4
18.	Does the supplier share quality data and histories with the customer?	X	__	4
19.	Are all quality data and results of performance measurements on file and current?	__	X	5
20.	Are defective material reports supplied to customer?	X	__	4

TOTAL POINTS (Record in "Points Awarded" column of Survey Scoring Summary): 83

Comments: While Five Star has sound Quality System, communication between functions could improve

CATEGORY 2: Total Cost

		YES	NO	POINTS
1.	Does the supplier have a cost accounting system which supports the pursuit of World Class status?	X	__	5
2.	Is supplier willing to share cost data with the customer, allowing the examination of historical, actual and projected cost data?	X	__	2
3.	Does the supplier track operating budgets and forecasts?	X	__	5
4.	Is the supplier willing to enter into long-term contracts and extend cost reductions to all partners?	__	X	1
5.	Does the supplier have an Activity Based Costing or total cost system?	X	__	4
6.	Is the supplier willing to commit to product life cycle costing?	X	__	5
7.	Does the supplier track performance against profitability goals?	X	__	5

8. Does the supplier track performance against contract terms?   X ___   5

9. Are the supplier's prices competitive?   X ___   3

10. Does percentage of goods and services sold to our company exceed 30% of total goods and services sold to all customers?   ___ X   4

11. Can the supplier demonstrate that there are teams actively working on cost reduction and waste elimination?   X ___   4

12. Does the supplier track the cost of quality?   X ___   2

13. Does the supplier have effective control of overtime?   X ___   3

14. Does the supplier have effective control of inventory?   X ___   3

15. Does the supplier have effective control of labor costs?   X ___   4

16. Can the supplier show that it is financially stable using generally accepted accounting principles as audited by an independent accounting firm?   X ___   5

17. Is the supplier able to demonstrate a trend of continuous sales and profitability growth over the past five years?   X ___   5

18. Has the supplier changed ownership or management frequently over the past five years?   X ___   5

19. Does the supplier have an adequate cash flow?   ___ X   4

20. Does the supplier have a history of frequent price increases?   X ___   4

TOTAL POINTS (Record in "Points Awarded" column of Survey Scoring Summary):   77

Comments: Good customer base, Needs to implement ABC more effectively

CATEGORY 3: Material Control

		YES	NO	POINTS
1.	Are storage areas adequately controlled and supervised?	X	__	4
2.	Is material segregated and identified by part number/customer/other?	X	__	4
3.	Is material with a limited shelf life clearly and accurately identified and controlled?	X	__	5
4.	Does the supplier have adequate procedures to detect and document transit damage, counts and correct deliveries?	X	__	5
5.	Are the procedures to assure proper storage conditions and to guard against damage from handling effectively employed?	X	__	4
6.	Are the procedures for identifying and tracing raw materials adequate?	X	__	4
7.	Does the supplier protect material from the environment?	X	__	4
8.	Does the supplier have an effective system of identifying and controlling in-process materials?	X	__	3
9.	Does the supplier have a fast and effective procedure for tracing and responding to customer inquiries?	X	__	5
10.	Is there a written procedure for receiving materials?	__	X	N/A
11.	Does the supplier have written procedures for the release of material to other departments, particularly manufacturing?	X	__	4
12.	Does the supplier have plans for the automation of material storage and retrieval? For example, Bar Coding.	X	__	5 Bar Coding
13.	Does the supplier have an effective inventory control program that seeks to maximize inventory turns?	X	__	4
14.	Does the supplier use physical inventories or cycle counts to ensure inventory accuracy? What is the current level of accuracy? __97__ %	X	__	5

	YES	NO	POINTS
15. Is there a formal routing method in place to ensure that materials are in the right place at the right time?	X		4
16. Is there a plan for reducing or eliminating surplus and obsolete inventories?	X		5
17. Does the supplier use or have EDI capability?		X	0
18. Does the supplier maintain data on its process capabilities?	X		5
19. Has the supplier put in place performance measurements for quality, on-time delivery and count accuracy?	X		4
20. Does the supplier communicate the results of performance measurements to its customers?	X		5

TOTAL POINTS (Record in "Points Awarded" column of Survey Scoring Summary)

79

Comments: Needs to implement EDI

CATEGORY 4: Process Control

	YES	NO	POINTS
1. Does the supplier use Statistical Process Control?	X		5
2. Is there a plan for preventive maintenance on equipment?	X		4
3. Is there evidence of a set-up reduction program?	X		3
4. Are drawing and specification changes well documented and controlled?	X		5
5. Does the supplier monitor work-in-process in order to maintain schedule adherence?	X		4
6. Does the supplier take effective corrective action in order to put production back on schedule if there is a slippage?	X		3
7. Does the supplier have an adequate procedure for managing capacity availability?	X		5

8. Is the Master Production Schedule centrally managed?	X __	4
9. Is there an ongoing program of education and training in process control for all levels of the organization?	X __	5
10. Is there a written procedure for process control that defines the methods of reporting and their frequency and timing?	X __	4
11. Is there a written procedure for process audits that defines the methods of reporting and their frequency and timing?	X __	3
12. Does the supplier have a written procedure that defines the methods for recording corrective actions and root causes?	X __	3
13. Are process controls set up at all critical points in the process?	X __	5
14. Is process control data prepared and distributed on a timely schedule to give advance warning of developing problems?	X __	5
15. Does the data show when the process is in control and when it is improving?	X __	5
16. Does the process control system trigger corrective action when the process is not in control limits?	X __	5
17. Are process changes controlled, authorized and documented?	X __	4
18. Is there evidence of a set-up reduction program to allow for quick change?	X __	3
19. Does the supplier use statistically designed experiments to solve quality problems and optimize process conditions for continuous quality improvement?	X __	4
20. Does the supplier use a "pull" vs. "push" technique to drive production?	X __	1

TOTAL POINTS (Record in "Points Awarded"
column of Survey Scoring Summary)   80

Comments: _____

CATEGORY 5: Safety and Housekeeping

	YES	NO	POINTS
1. Are all areas of the plant kept clean and free of nonessential items?	X	__	4
2. How safe are manufacturing work areas? (Proper ventilation, good lighting, safe noise levels, safety glasses, etc.)	X	__	4
3. Does the plant monitor compliance to regulatory agencies? (OSHA, EPA, etc.)	X	__	5
4. Does the supplier have a preventive maintenance program in place for both the equipment and the facilities?	X	__	4
5. Are there regular safety inspections?	X	__	3
6. Is there an education and training program in place for employees to learn good safety and housekeeping practices?	X	__	3
7. Are the facilities and equipment in good working order?	X	__	4
8. Does all transportation comply with established vehicle safety standards?	X	__	3
9. Is there a written safety program?	X	__	5
10. Are housekeeping audits conducted on a regular schedule?	X	__	4
11. Does the supplier have a written procedure for reporting deviations from preventive maintenance standards?	X	__	5
12. Do safety and housekeeping procedures comply with industry standards?	X	__	5
13. Does the supplier have a formal safety review program?	X	__	3
14. Does the supplier take timely corrective action when an accident occurs?	X	__	5
15. Are safety and housekeeping incidents thoroughly documented?	X	__	5
16. Are there written safety instructions for special or dangerous procedures?	X	__	5
17. Are there written housekeeping instructions for special or dangerous procedures?	X	__	4

	YES	NO	POINTS
18. Does the supplier have a policy in which all employees are responsible for preventive maintenance?	X		2
19. Are preventive maintenance records available for customer perusal?		X	5
20. Does management support safety and housekeeping efforts?	X		5

TOTAL POINTS (Record in "Points Awarded" column of Survey Scoring Summary)   83

Comments: Clean facility. PM done by maint. team.

No TQM presently.

CATEGORY 6: Documentation and Record Control

	YES	NO	POINTS
1. Is documentation accurate and current?	X		5
2. Does the supplier have a positive recall system to find up-to-date procedures, specifications and drawings?	X		5
3. Are records kept of inspections and process control?	X		5
4. Is there a procedure in place for the distribution of documents?	X		3
5. Are obsolete specifications, procedures, requirements and drawings purged from the system?	X		5
6. Are proposed changes communicated to all departments needing the information?	X		4
7. Are proposed changes communicated to the customer?	X		5
8. Are test procedures readily available for review?	X		5

		YES	NO	POINTS
9.	Does the supplier have a list of documents to be controlled?	X		5
10.	Has the supplier defined a retention time for records?	X		3
11.	Is there a back-up system in place?	X		2
12.	Are records stored in a safe and secure location?			
13.	Have procedures been put in place to protect against computer tampering or sabotage?	X		2
		X		3
14.	Have procedures been put in place to protect against computer viruses?	X		4
15.	Are all associated employees trained in the document and record control system?	X		3
16.	Is the system audited on a periodic basis?	X		3
17.	Are the results of these audits available for review by customers?	X		5
18.	Does the supplier have a system of controlled access?	X		4
19.	Is the supplier ISO 9000 registered?		X	1 Beginning
20.	Does management support documentation and record control efforts?	X		5

TOTAL POINTS (Record in "Points Awarded" column of Survey Scoring Summary)   77

Comments: Working toward ISO. Backup procedures need improvement

CATEGORY 7: Organization and Administration

		YES	NO	POINTS
1.	Is area performance communicated to management on a regular basis?	X		4
2.	Is management receptive to new ideas and changes in order to ensure continuous improvement?	X		5

3. Does management support a partnership relationship with customers and suppliers?   X ___   5

4. Is the supplier's organizational structure documented?   X ___   3

5. Has management identified and implemented employee education and training programs for the acquisition of World Class skills?   X ___   3

6. Does the supplier have an employee involvement program in place?   X ___   5

7. Is the supplier moving toward being able to compete in an agile business environment?   X ___   2

8. Has management identified a business plan describing commitments of capital and resources?   X ___   5

9. Is the supplier's organizational structure well defined?   X ___   5

10. Does the supplier have a program for reducing cycle time?   X ___   4

11. Does the supplier regularly communicate performance result to employees?   X ___   4

12. Does the supplier use the results of internal audits to initiate corrective actions?   X ___   4

13. Does supplier notify customers of potential nonconformances or late deliveries in advance of the scheduled due date?   X ___   5

14. Does the supplier regularly visit suppliers and customers to solicit input?   X ___   5

15. Are administrative and product/service quality systems given equal weight?   X ___   4

16. Is supplier involved in professional or industry organizations?   X ___   5

17. Does the supplier's mission statement reflect customer requirements?   X ___   5

18. Has the supplier made it clear to all levels that quality is everybody's responsibility?   X ___   4

19. Does the organization or administration of the supplier's company impede change?   X ___   5

20. Does the supplier's management actively look to embrace appropriate new technologies?   X __   5

TOTAL POINTS (Record in "Points Awarded" column of Survey Scoring Summary)   87

Comments: Management actively involved in CIP

CATEGORY 8: Customer Service and Satisfaction

	YES	NO	POINTS
1. Are employees courteous and knowledgeable?	X	__	5
2. Does the supplier respond to inquiries in less than 24 hours?	X	__	5
3. Does the supplier handle claims objectively and promptly?	X	__	4
4. Does the supplier provide technical and commercial assistance for both new and existing products?	X	__	4
5. Is the supplier willing to listen to recommendations for usage and improvement?	X	__	5
6. Is the supplier able to demonstrate a customer service function with a clearly defined organization?	X	__	4
7. Does the supplier measure the performance of customer service?	X	__	5
8. Does the supplier measure the customer satisfaction level?	X	__	5
9. Is the supplier's management actively involved in achieving customer satisfaction?	X	__	4
10. Is the supplier's level of customer service comparable to its competition's?	X	__	5
11. Does the supplier regularly communicate per-formance results to employees?	X	__	3

	YES	NO	POINTS
12. Does the supplier have teams in place to direct the achievement of continuous improvement in customer service?	X	__	2
13. Has the supplier established World Class goals?	X	__	4
14. Does the supplier regularly visit customers to solicit input?	X	__	5
15. Does the supplier have a documented procedure for handling customer complaints?	X	__	5
16. Are records kept of complaints and are they used to drive corrective action?	X	__	4
17. Can customer service personnel resolve complaints without seeking management approval?	X	__	5
18. Has the supplier made it clear to all levels that service is everybody's responsibility?	X	__	5
19. Does the supplier provide adequate field support?	X	__	4
20. Does the supplier strictly enforce ethical business practices?	X	__	5

TOTAL POINTS (Record in "Points Awarded" column of Survey Scoring Summary)   88

Comments:: Respond very well and in a timely fashion

CATEGORY 9: Information Management

	YES	NO	POINTS
1. Does the supplier have clearly defined information management policies and procedures?	X	__	4
2. Is the phasing in of new information management technologies done in a proscribed, formal manner?	X	__	4

3. Does the supplier solicit input from customers when planning new information management procedures?   X ___   5

4. Are there procedures in place for translating customer requirements into design requirements?   X ___   5

5. Has management identified and implementedemployee education and training programs for the acquisition of World Class skills?   X ___   4

6. Are all information management requirements documented and maintained in an accurate and timely fashion?   X ___   4

7. Does the supplier have a system for tracking the development of its information management system?   X ___   3

8. Has management identified information management requirements in its business plan?   X ___   4

9. Is the information management function's organizational structure well defined?   X ___   5

10. Does the supplier employ all relevant industry standards?   X ___   5

11. Does the supplier measure performance and report results to employees?   X ___   4

12. Does the supplier use measurement results to initiate corrective actions?   X ___   5

13. Does supplier notify customers of potential nonconformances?   X ___   5

14. Is there a documented procedure for releasing updates to the information management system?   X ___   5

15. Is there a documented procedure for releasing changes to the information management system?   X ___   5

16. Is the testing of the information management system done independently?   X ___   5

17. Does the supplier create testing conditions similar to actual working conditions?   X ___   4

18. Is the supplier's information manage-
    ment system compatible with our
    system?   X __   5
19. Does the supplier have EDI capability?   X __   5
20. Does the supplier's management
    actively look to embrace appropriate
    new technologies?   X __   5

**TOTAL POINTS (Record in "Points
Awarded" column of Survey Scoring
Summary)**   88

Comments: System flow within guidelines expected by us

CATEGORY 10: Supply Management

		YES	NO	POINTS

1. Does the supplier base its method for
   selecting its own suppliers onprocess
   control, quality and delivery ratings?   X __   5
2. Is there a documented procedure for
   tracking nonconformances?   X __   5
3. Does management support a partner-
   ship relationship with its suppliers?   X __   3
4. Are the sub-tier suppliers' facilities
   geographically close to major trans-
   portation arteries?   X __   2
5. Have sub-tier suppliers implemented
   employee education and training
   programs for the acquisition of World
   Class skills?   X __   1
6. Do sub-tier suppliers have employee
   involvement programs in place?   X __   1
7. Are sub-tier suppliers moving toward
   being able to compete in an agile
   business environment?   X __   2
8. Do sub-tier suppliers use a system to
   track on-time delivery to the sup-
   plier?   X __   5

9. Is the supplier's responsibility for logistics well defined?   X ___   4

10. Do the sub-tier suppliers have a program for reducing cycle time?   X ___   3

11. Does the sub-tier supplier regularly communicate performance results to its customers?   X ___   5

12. Does the sub-tier supplier use the results of internal audits to initiate corrective actions?   X ___   4

13. Does the sub-tier supplier notify customers of potential nonconformances or late deliveries in advance of the scheduled due date?   X ___   5

14. Does the supplier regularly visit sub-tier suppliers to solicit input?   X ___   5

15. Does the supplier review freight costs on a regular basis?   X ___   4

16. Is the sub-tier supplier involved in professional or industry organizations?   X ___   2

17. Does the sub-tier supplier's mission statement reflect customer requirements?   X ___   4

18. Has the sub-tier supplier made it clear to all levels that quality is everybody's responsibility?   X ___   4

19. Does the organization or administration of the sub-tier supplier's company impede change?   X ___   4

20. Does the sub-tier supplier's management actively look to embrace appropriate new technologies?   X ___   3

TOTAL POINTS (Record in "Points Awarded" column of Survey Scoring Summary):   71

Comments: Many sub-tier suppliers are small with little financial support

CATEGORY 11: Design and Product Development

		YES	NO	POINTS

Comments:

		YES	NO	POINTS
1.	Is the supplier's system of managing and storing customer supplied design documentation effective?	X	__	5
2.	Is the supplier's change control process for customer initiated revisions reliable?	X	__	4
3.	Is customer documentation distributed internally to all departments that require the information?	X	__	5
4.	Does the supplier have an effective system of notifying customers of design problems?	X	__	3
5.	Has the supplier implemented employee education and training programs for the acquisition of World Class skills?	X	__	4
6.	Does the supplier have employee involvement programs in place?	X	__	4
7.	Is the supplier moving toward being able to compete in an agile business environment?	X	__	4
8.	Does the supplier document the solutions to design problems and use them for continuous improvement?	X	__	5
9.	Is the supplier's disaster recovery capability adequate?	X	__	4
10.	Is the supplier working on new product development for future needs?	X	__	N/A
11.	Is there a system in place for monitoring the effectiveness and timeliness of design activities?	X	__	3
12.	Are computer design tools used in the design of new products, technologies	X	__	N/A

or services?

	YES	NO	POINTS
13. Are statistical tools used in the development of new products, technologies or services?	X	__	N/A
14. Is there a policy for patents and are any pending?	X	__	N/A
15. Does the supplier have a long-term technology plan?	X	__	4
16. Are a sufficient number of employees involved in professional or industry organizations?	X	__	5
17. Is the process for designing and developing new products, technologies or services fully documented to ensure reproducibility?	X	__	N/A
18. Does the supplier establish specific quality objectives in the design of new products, technologies or services?	X	__	3
19. Does the supplier review the design process on a periodic basis?	X	__	5
20. Does the supplier use Concurrent Engineering?	X	__	5

TOTAL POINTS (Record in "Points Awarded" column of Survey Scoring Summary):   63

Comments: Product designs are suggested. Product Development

            not applicable. Need CAD/CAM.

CATEGORY 12: Capacity

	YES	NO	POINTS
1. Does the supplier have documented process plans?	X	__	5
2. Does the supplier have the appropriate diversification of equipment to produce our planned products?	X	__	3

3.	Are the employees qualified to perform their job functions?	X ___	5
4.	Does the supplier have a set-up/queue reduction program in place?	X ___	5
5.	Has the supplier implemented employee education and training programs for the acquisition of World Class skills?	X ___	4
6.	Does supplier have employee involvement programs in place?	X ___	5
7.	Is the supplier moving toward being able to compete in an agile business environment?	X ___	3
8.	Does the supplier have a capacity planning/tracking system in place?	X ___	5
9.	Does the supplier use the capacity planning/tracking system to determine availability of capacity to accept purchase order delivery dates?	X ___	4
10.	Does the supplier conduct regular reviews of process capability?	X ___	5
11.	Are the results of these reviews forwarded to Design Engineering to be used in product development?	X ___	2
12.	Does the supplier use problem-solving tools to identify and resolve capacity problems?	X ___	5
13.	Is there a program in place to reduce process variability?	X ___	5
14.	Are statistical techniques used to measure process capability against product specifications?	X ___	5
15.	Are written procedures provided to operators to prevent the process from moving out of control?	X ___	5
16.	Does the supplier solicit input from customers?	X ___	5

		YES	NO	POINTS
17.	Does the supplier obtain process capability studies from sub-tier suppliers?	X	__	1
18.	Is there a documented calibration system with periodic audits?	X	__	5
19.	Are final acceptance procedures documented, controlled and followed?	X	__	5
20.	Are lots kept intact and traceable throughout the process?	X	__	4

TOTAL POINTS (Record in "Points Awarded" column of Survey Scoring Summary):   86

Comments: Capacity planning/tracking well organized

Need CPK from suppliers

CATEGORY 13: Delivery and Shipping

		YES	NO	POINTS
1.	Is there same day pull of orders?	X	__	4
2.	Is there shipment of open orders within one working day?	X	__	3
3.	Are orders 100% accurate?	X	__	4
4.	Are deliveries 100% on-time?	__	X	3
5.	Has the supplier implemented employee education and training programs for the acquisition of World Class skills?	X	__	4
6.	Does the supplier monitor on-time delivery performance?	X	__	5
7.	Does the supplier maintain packaging specifications in an effective manner?	X	__	4
8.	Are there written procedures for packaging products?	X	__	5
9.	Are customer traffic and routing instructions visible in the shipping area?	X	__	4

10.	Are there written procedures for including proper enclosures with each shipment?	X ___	5
11.	Are there written procedures for shipping hazardous materials?	X ___	5
12.	Does the supplier have bar coding capability?	X ___	5
13.	Does the supplier notify customers of potential nonconformances or late deliveries in advance of the scheduled due date?	X ___	5
14.	Does the supplier have agreements with freight carriers that ensure on-time delivery?	___ X	4
15.	Are proper customer codes and labels attached to each shipment?	X ___	5
16.	Are approved lots kept intact in the shipping and packaging processes?	X ___	4
17.	Is nonconforming material properly identified and segregated?	X ___	4
18.	Does the supplier have ship-direct capabilities?	X ___	5
19.	Does the supplier have a shelf-life program for products?	X ___	4
20.	Does the supplier have written agreements with transport companies for the return of defective goods?	___ X	3

TOTAL POINTS (Record in "Points Awarded" column of Survey Scoring Summary):

85

Comments: Backlog exists for shipping, preventing 100% on time

CATEGORY 14: GMP, Labor Relations, and Regulatory Compliance

	YES	NO	POINTS
1. Does the supplier understand and use Good Manufacturing Practices?	X		5
2. Is the supplier in compliance with right-to-know laws?	X		5
3. Does management support a partnership relationship with its supplier	X		5
4. Has the supplier been cited by any agency for violations?		X	5
5. Does the supplier have a published code of ethics?	X		5
6. Does the supplier have a published policy on conflicts of interest?	X		4
7. Is there evidence of open lines of communication between management and employees?	X		4
8. Is there an established mandatory training program in the handling of dangerous goods?	X		5
9. Are there published emergency response procedures and guidelines?	X		5
10. Is the supplier in compliance with regulatory agencies?	X		5
11. Is compliance monitored and controlled?	X		4
12. Does the supplier promote the use of employee involvement and empowerment programs?	X		4
13. Are cross-functional teams used for problem solving?	X		4
14. Does the supplier provide education and training for all employees at every level?	X		4
15. Is the supplier an equal opportunity employer?	X		5

16. Has the supplier experienced any work stoppages in the last three years? ___ _X_ _4_

17. Have labor disputes been settled without resorting to outside mediation? _X_ ___ _5_

18. Has the supplier made it clear to all levels that they have the responsibility and authority to achieve continuous improvement? _X_ ___ _4_

19. Does the organization or administration of the supplier impede change? ___ _X_ _4_

20. Does the supplier have an equal or better than industry average for employee turnover rate, absenteeism, productivity, and advancement? _X_ ___ _3_

TOTAL POINTS (Record in "Points Awarded" column of Survey Scoring Summary): 89

Comments: _____

SUMMARY SHEET

Ques.	Section													
	1	2	3	4	5	6	7	8	9	10	11	12	13	14
1	4	4	4	5	4	5	4	5	4	5	5	5	4	5
2	5	5	4	4	4	5	5	5	4	5	4	3	3	5
3	5	2	5	3	5	5	5	4	5	3	5	5	4	5
4	4	5	5	5	4	3	3	4	5	2	3	5	3	5
5	5	1	4	4	3	5	3	5	4	1	4	4	4	5
6	3	4	4	3	3	4	5	4	4	1	4	5	5	4
7	4	5	4	5	4	5	2	5	3	2	4	3	4	4
8	3	5	3	4	3	5	5	5	4	5	5	5	5	5
9	4	3	5	5	5	5	5	4	5	4	4	4	4	5
10	4	4	N/A	4	4	3	4	5	5	3	N/A	5	5	5
11	4	4	4	3	5	2	4	3	4	5	3	2	5	4
12	4	2	5	3	5	2	4	2	5	4	N/A	5	5	4
13	5	3	4	5	3	3	5	4	5	5	N/A	5	5	4
14	4	3	5	5	5	4	5	5	5	5	N/A	5	4	4
15	5	4	4	5	5	3	4	5	4	4	4	5	5	5
16	3	5	5	5	5	3	5	4	3	2	5	5	4	4
17	4	5	0	4	4	5	5	5	5	4	N/A	1	4	5
18	4	5	5	3	2	4	4	5	5	4	3	5	5	4
19	5	4	4	4	5	1	5	4	5	4	5	5	4	4
20	4	4	5	1	5	5	5	5	4	3	5	4	3	3
Total Pts.	83	77	79	80	83	77	87	88	88	71	63	86	85	89

Type of Supplier: _____ Mfg. _____

QUALIFICATION SURVEY SUMMARY

Company Name	Five Star Manufacturing	**Surveyed By**	Manufacturing Commodity Team
Address	PO Box 1403	**Accompanied By**	Accounting
City, State, Zip	Marshville, IL 33407-1917	(**Initial Survey**)	**Resurvey**
Phone	407-257-8699	**Survey Date**	9/10/96
Supplier Code	Five Star	**Contact**	Robert Vance
Supplier Score	80.8	**Minimum Required Score: 65**	

RECOMMENDATIONS

Supplier has potential to become a critical partner. However, limited design/development capability prevents continued growth. Five Star will embark on implementing and upgrading design/development function for our business.

ACTION PLAN IS DUE BY: _____ 11/10/96 _____

SUPPLIER ACKNOWLEDGMENT:

_____   9/10/96

Signature   *Date*

TYPES
OF
AUDITS

CHAPTER SIX

Types of Audits

◊ Suitability vs. conformity

◊ Process

◊ Systems

◊ Effects on programs

◊ Measurements of compliance

◊ Quality

◊ Performance

◊ Total cost

◊ Good Manufacturing Practices

Suitability Audit

Evaluation and comparison of a quality program (documentation) against a reference standard.

Process Quality Audit

◊   Identify players

◊   Establish a date

◊   Create an agenda

Quality Level Based On:

◊   Management's desire

◊   Marketplace needs

◊   National standards

◊   Procurement standards – major customers

◊   GMP via regulatory agencies

◊   Specific requirements of products and services

DOCUMENTATION OF A QUALITY SYS-TEM ENSURES THAT A PROGRAM WORKS TOWARD A COMMON SET OF RULES!

Quality Systems Audit

    ◊   Suitabilty for adherence to system requirements

    ◊   Conformity for effectiveness of activities

Quality Programs Include

    ◊   Policies

    ◊   Procedures

    ◊   Operating instructions

    ◊   Purpose to achieve a desired quality level

Quality System

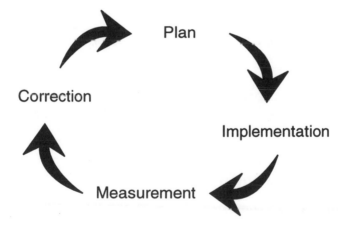

Plan

Implementation

Measurement

Correction

Good Manufacturing Practices (GMP)

Good Manufacturing Practices (GMP) were developed to assist manufacturers in regulated industries complete, maintain or expand their quality assurance programs. These regulations are flexible. They specify general objectives rather than specific procedures. Of particular importance are:

◊ issues with nonconformance.

◊ regulatory practices.

◊ work instructions.

◊ housekeeping.

◊ hazardous material control.

◊ safety and health.

A GMP program falls in between Quality Control and Total Quality Assurance (TQA). GMP assures that the end product meets its design specifications. That is a significant step up from Quality Control. However, GMP lacks methods to improve a poor design. The differences between GMP and TQA are shown in the table on the next page.

Compliance With GMP

◊ Master records

◊ History records

◊ Maintenance schedules and records

◊ Complaint files (failed devices/components)

	GMP SYSTEM	TQA SYSTEM
Customer Needs		X
Design		X
Design Evaluation		X
Design of Packaging, Labels	X	X
Design Transfer	X	X
Manufacturing, Control	X	X
Packaging, Labels, Distribution	X	X
Installation	X	X
Complaints	X	X
Repairs		X

◊ Audit reports

◊ Distribution and training records

Documentation Requirements for GMP

◊ Written inspection procedures

◊ Testing procedures

◊ Calibration and maintenance procedures

Audits and Surveys for Adherence

◊ Assurance procedures are performed

◊ Accountability

◊ Minimum requirements

SURVEY
PROCEDURES
AND
POLICIES

CHAPTER SEVEN

Survey Procedures

1. Contact supplier
2. Send out presurvey
3. Prepare for survey
4. Define responsibility and authority
5. Methodology
6. Proactive programs – internal and external
7. Certification programs

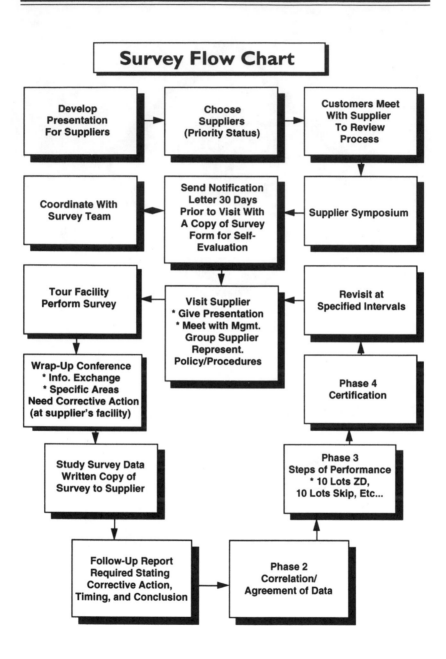

Survey Flow Chart

Develop Presentation For Suppliers	Choose Suppliers (Priority Status)	Customers Meet With Supplier To Review Process
Coordinate With Survey Team	Send Notification Letter 30 Days Prior to Visit With A Copy of Survey Form for Self-Evaluation	Supplier Symposium
Tour Facility Perform Survey	Visit Supplier * Give Presentation * Meet with Mgmt. Group Supplier Represent. Policy/Procedures	Revisit at Specified Intervals
Wrap-Up Conference * Info. Exchange * Specific Areas Need Corrective Action (at supplier's facility)		Phase 4 Certification
Study Survey Data Written Copy of Survey to Supplier		Phase 3 Steps of Performance * 10 Lots ZD, 10 Lots Skip, Etc...
Follow-Up Report Required Stating Corrective Action, Timing, and Conclusion	Phase 2 Correlation/ Agreement of Data	

Preparation for Survey

1. Do we conduct a survey? Yes or no?
2. Contact education (supplier).
3. Advance view of survey.
4. Identify players.
5. Establish a date.
6. Create an agenda.

Each survey should have a time set aside for a Pre-Team Meeting. This will allow for preparation up front.

1. Discuss format/agenda for survey.
2. Review checklist, if needed.
3. Gain familiarity with materials purchased from suppliers.
4. Review raw material for supplier profile.
5. Understand supplier's production process.
6. Review past performance.
7. Review test results/specifications from incoming test.
8. Review previous survey if applicable.
9. Gain familiarity with a contract (if any) with the supplier.
10. Collect information from local experts.

At a minimum, these ten points must be discussed. We propose you send the supplier a criteria list prior to the visit.

What other issues would you want to discuss?

☑ _____

_____

_____

Responsibility and Authority

Survey Team:

◊ Each member must be from respective, functional areas

◊ Verify documentation

◊ Decision maker

◊ Company being surveyed: _____

◊ Counterparts

◊ Make changes happen

◊ Supported by top management

Methodology

Opening Meeting:

◊ Meet players/top management.

◊ Plant team.

◊ Restate survey objectives.

◊ Identify logistics (conference rooms).

Checklist

◊ Take breaks after each section.

◊ Contract the process.

◊ Have working lunches.

◊ Look for measurements.

◊ Complete verification of completeness.

◊ Check notes.

◊ Identify the not applicable.

◊ Conduct survey on their offices.

◊ Take good notes.

◊ Follow example through process.

◊ Expand questions.

◊ Summarize with suppliers.

Suggested Agenda – Supplier Survey

Location: _____

Date: _____

Survey Team: _____

9:00 - 9:15	Arrival - Introductions
9:16 - 9:45	Opening Remarks - Review of Objectives * Supplier and Company
9:46 - 10:45	Plant Tour
10:46 - 11:15	Raw Materials - Receiving, Testing, Storage, and Release to Manufacturers * Supplier Presentation by Appropriate Person(s)

11:16 - 11:45	Manufacturing Record Retention and Control * Supplier Presentation by Appropriate Person(s)
11:46 - 12:15	Manufacturing Operation - Calibration and Preventive Maintenance * Supplier Presentation by Appropriate Person(s)
12:16 - 12:45	Process Control * Supplier Presentation by Appropriate Person(s)
12:46 - 1:15	Nonconforming Product and Corrective Action System * Supplier Presentation by Appropriate Person(s)
1:16 - 1:45	Quality Control * Supplier Presentation by Appropriate Person(s)
1:46 - 2:15	Packing and Shipping * Supplier Presentation by Appropriate Person(s)
2:16 - 2:45	Safety and Housekeeping * Supplier Presentation by Appropriate Person(s)
2:46 - 3:15	Management * General Discussion Between Supplier and Company
3:16 - 3:45	Wrap-up Discussion

A working lunch would be fine. Without a working lunch, please add the appropriate one hour to the suggested schedule.

Definitions

Customer - Supplier Relationship

Because raw materials are major components of all processes, they can be a significant source of both process bias and assignable cause variation. It is highly desirable to consider the raw materials supplier as a partner and develop a cooperative relationship. A confrontational relationship benefits neither the customer nor the supplier.

Supplier Quality Survey

Supplier quality surveys are an important tool in the establishment, measurement, maintenance, and improvement of raw material quality. A survey is the objective quantized measurement of a supplier's capability to supply raw materials that meet specified requirements. The intent of the survey is to determine areas of opportunity and improvement.

Verifying the system and process provides a sound foundation for the visit. Separation of trivial from improvement issues comes from proper weighing of the survey. A factory tour must meet the criteria established.

◊   Internal process

◊   Separate important from trivial

◊   Identify where activity takes place

◊   "Smell the factory"

A proactive quality program and process should:

◊   have a design that helps satisfy quality objectives.

◊   provide resources.

◊   anticipate problems and control.

•   employ process control

•   know rights

•   process capability

•   start a process which meets requirements

•   verify performance

•   improve process to reduce dispositions of results

Sources of Facts

◊   Physical check

◊   Confirmation

◊   Tangible conclusion(s)/symptoms via

•   tracing

•   sampling

•   correlation

PERFORMANCE MEASUREMENTS

CHAPTER EIGHT

How do we know if we are succeeding? That is the question that must be addressed. We measure performance in order to be predictable, so that we know where we have been, where we are, and where we are going. It is possible to measure the wrong areas.

The problem with the old yardstick of performance is that they are not looking at solutions. They look only at productivity levels and use a reactive, rather than a proactive approach.

Today, we must use new yardsticks which provide information to make decisions. Then, we will be able to compare actual data against predicted performance. This gives us the opportunity to take corrective action. This is the definition of proactive: to measure the predictability of the outcomes of decision-making in real time.

This is best accomplished through a system of measurement that reflects a Total Business Concept. In general, the use of TBC measurements will show:

1. how close we are to having on-line, real-time information about both internal and external manufacturing operations as well as purchasing activities. Current supplier involvement will provide a new approach.

2. how accurate our information is. We all know that a small mistake compounds over time. Unlike interest on your personal investments, this is not favorable. The surveyor who makes a mistake of one degree can cost you many valuable acres of land.

3. how much waste is present in manufacturing and supplier operations and purchasing activities. Waste, today, is too often accepted as a given and absorbed into overhead costs. This is truly a reactive way of thinking and must change as we compete in a world market.

4. how actual performance compares to the stated plan. Observing this variance is instrumental in making new plans which take corrective action. Those who don't learn from the mistakes of the past are DOOMED to repeat them.

Performance measurements can include utilizing a standard, supplier evaluation or pass/fail criteria. Additional measurements include set-up reduction, ship to work-in-process, on time delivery, and quality.

However, successful implementation of any measurement strategy begins with establishing a baseline. This will serve as a mark to measure progress against. When rushing to implement a new business/management strategy, may companies overlook this vitally important step.

Companies enthusiastically embrace the continuous improvement plan. Not long after implementation, they become lost. A member of the company's "exploration" team pulls out a "map" and begins examining it.

"Where are we," asks another team member after a few minutes.

The person looks up from the map and points to a mountain visible on the horizon. "See that mountain over there? From what I can tell, we're on top of it."

This illustrates what happens when companies fail to determine their present status as a benchmark for measuring their future progress. Companies can use surveys to gather information about the suppliers' current position in order to establish a baseline. Audits can then be used to reexamine the areas with deficiencies. Any improvements are clearly seen when compared to the benchmark.

Supplier Measurement Reference Standards

◊   Meet business expectations.

◊   Obtain quantitative measures.

◊   Establish a benchmark.

◊   Accumulate subsequent data.

◊   Compare results and search/analyze for causes or shortcomings.

◊ Continue to provide information toward achieving Continuous Improvement.

In selecting a supplier in an attempt to optimize profits, don't focus on just price. Quality, quantity, and delivery are also important factors to consider.

THE RIGHT ITEM, IN THE RIGHT PLACE, AT THE RIGHT TIME, IN THE RIGHT QUANTITY, AND MEETING CUSTOMER REQUIREMENTS EVERY TIME AND EVERYWHERE IN THE COMPANY AT THE LOWEST TOTAL COST.

Utilize The Score From The Survey

◊ Prior qualification

◊ Establish pass/fail

◊ What should the criteria be?

Findings

◊ How much variation should be allowed?

◊ How rigid should you be?

◊ Small vs. large organizations

THE SUPPLIER/CUSTOMER ASSESSMENT

CHAPTER NINE

Eliminating waste and inspection are the premier goals of supplier surveys and audits. Other important goals are similar to those of JIT (Just-In-Time) and TQC (Total Quality Control). Both address the elimination of waste and both give a win/win mentality. What's good for you is good for your supplier. What you expect from your supplier, you should expect from your own company. In fact, it is because of the philosophy "the right product in the right place at the right time."

Goal	Action
Total Quality Control	Ensure that the entire manufacturing cycle from design review through customer receipt meets quality standards established by the customer.

Goal	Action
Quantity	Process and produce the lowest possible quantity by manufacturing on time. The smaller the quantity, the easier it is to control.
Supplier Partnership	Establish a relationship based on a win/win philosophy.
Logistics	Simplify the control and movement of material between functions and activities, incorporate standard objectives.

Closure/Action

◊ Policy and objective

◊ Corrective action

◊ Supplier response/concerns

◊ Provide client/supplier status

◊ Initiate corrective action

The final checkpoint is to perform an analysis, assign responsibility and authority.

◊ Identifies ownership/responsibility

◊ Equipment/process

◊ Correct designs

◊ Training needs

Corrective Action Worksheet

To _____

Location _____

Date _____

Product/Process_____

Problem _____

_____

_____

The Quality Survey has made the following observations in your area of concern. Action is requested to correct these observations and prevent recurrence of them.

Requirement _____

_____

Observation _____

_____

Action is required by _____

_____

The following actions have been taken to correct this occurrence and to prevent recurrence. _____

_____

Signed _____   Date _____

Position_____

The actions taken are   Acceptable / Not Acceptable

Signed _____   Date _____

        Quality Survey Manager

Further Action_____

Response To Evaluation

◊ Identify the root cause(s)

◊ The Five W's

Closing The Loop

◊ Feedback (acceptable, timetable, result orientation)

◊ Identification (root cause and effect)

◊ Maintenance of the relationship (ongoing audit & frequency schedule)

◊ People (empowerment)

◊ Suppliers (responsibility and involvement)

Partnership Performance Survey

In a true partnership, both parties must be open to continuous improvement. The customer should therefore be responsive to surveys/audits by their supplier.

Some supplier to customer questions/concerns:

◊ Purchase order/EDI accuracy

◊ Drawing specification and change notices accuracy/timeline

◊ Communication

◊ Information sharing

◊ Market intelligence/research

What category types/criteria and questions do you think your suppliers could ask your company to answer/respond to?

☑ _____

_____

_____

Which could potentially improve your operations?

☑ _____

_____

_____

SUPPLIER CERTIFICATION

CHAPTER TEN

The flow chart on the following page depicts the steps in the supplier certification process and shows where supplier surveys and audits falls within that process.

Process Quality Standards

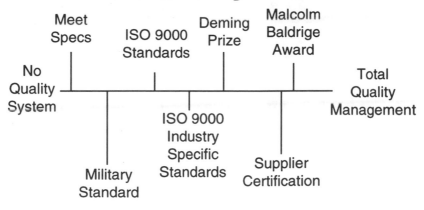

Supplier Certification Flowchart

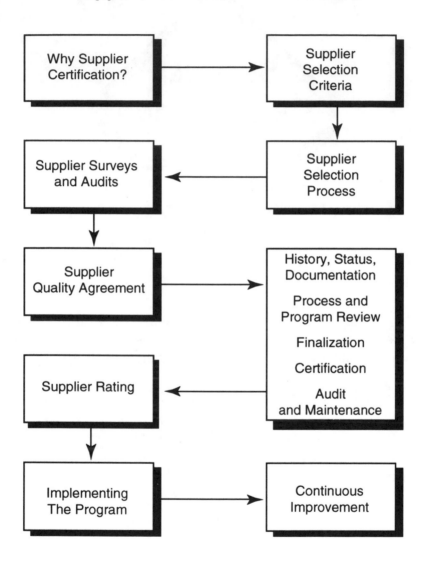

What is ISO?

The International Organization for Standardization (ISO) is the specialized international agency for standardization. Currently the standards of 91 countries are embodied in ISO.

The objective of ISO is to promote the development of standardization of world activities with a view to facilitating the international exchange of goods and services.

Although these standards are not the same as certification, any supplier that meets these standards should be considered a very eligible candidate for certification. However, certification to the standard will be required to ship to Europe.

ISO Requirements

◊   Documented quality systems

◊   Procedures, manuals, instructions

◊   Management's total support

◊   Organization goals and objectives

Baldrige Award Criteria Framework Dynamic Relationships

Goals:

◊   Customer satisfaction

◊   Customer satisfaction relative to competitors

◊   Market share

Measures of Progress:

◊   Product & service quality

◊   Internal quality and productivity

◊   Supplier quality

Core Values And Concepts:

These are designed, according to the Award Criteria booklet, to "address and integrate the overall customer and company performance requirements." You will notice that the Baldrige core values and concepts are similar to the core concepts of a successful supplier certification program.

◊   Customer-driven quality

◊   Leadership

◊   Continuous improvement

◊   Full participation

◊   Fast response

◊   Design quality and prevention

◊   Long-range outlook

◊   Management by fact

◊   Partnership development

◊   Public response

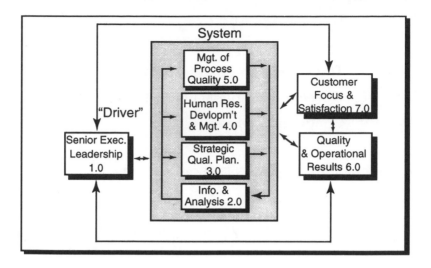

Key Characteristics Of The Criteria:

The criteria:

◊ are directed toward producing results.

◊ are nonprescriptive.

◊ link process to results.

◊ are part of a diagnostic system.

◊ are comprehensive.

◊ include key learning cycles.

◊ emphasize quality system alignment.

The Next Step

◊ Establish a team.

◊ Educate the resources.

◊   Develop a presurvey.

◊   Develop survey(s).

◊   Test survey (internal/external).

◊   Develop an implementation plan.

◊   Conduct the survey(s).

Supplier Certification References from PT Publications, Inc.

Supplier Certification II: A Handbook for Achieving Excellence through Continuous Improvement
   Peter L. Grieco, Jr.

Supply Management Toolbox: How to Manage Your Suppliers
   Peter L. Grieco, Jr.

Supplier Certification: The Path to Excellence Video Education Series

Tape 1: *Why Supplier Certification?*	$395.00
Tape 2: *Quality at the Supplier*	$395.00
Tape 3: *How to Select a Supplier*	$395.00
Tape 4: *Supplier Surveys and Audits*	$395.00
Tape 5: *Supplier Quality Agreements*	$395.00
Tape 6: *Supplier Ratings*	$395.00
Tape 7: *Phases of Supplier Certification*	$395.00
Tape 8: *Implementing a Supplier Cert. Program*	$395.00
Tape 9: *Evaluating Your Supplier Cert. Program*	$395.00
Complete Nine Tape Series	$1,995.00

ADDITIONAL PURCHASING RESOURCES

FROM PT PUBLICATIONS, INC.

3109 45th Street, Suite 100
West Palm Beach, FL 33407-1915
1-800-272-4335

THE PURCHASING ENCYCLOPEDIA

Just-In-Time Purchasing: In Pursuit of Excellence $29.95
    Peter L. Grieco, Jr., Michael W. Gozzo
    & Jerry W. Claunch

Glossary of Key Purchasing Terms, Acronyms, and Formulas PT Publications	$14.95
Supplier Certification II: A Handbook for Achieving Excellence through Continuous Improvement Peter L. Grieco, Jr.	$49.95
World Class: Measuring Its Achievement Peter L. Grieco, Jr.	$39.95
Purchasing Performance Measurements: A Roadmap For Excellence Mel Pilachowski	$12.95
The World Of Negotiations: Never Being a Loser Peter L. Grieco, Jr. and Paul G. Hine	$39.95
How To Conduct Supplier Surveys and Audits Janet L. Przirembel	$14.95
Supply Management Toolbox: How to Manage Your Suppliers Peter L. Grieco, Jr.	$26.95
Purchasing Capital Equipment Thomas E. Petroski	$14.95
Power Purchasing: Supply Management in in the 21st Century Peter L. Grieco, Jr. and Carl R. Cooper	$39.95
Global Sourcing Lee Krotseng	$14.95
Purchasing Contract Law, UCC, and Patents Mark Grieco	$14.95
EDI Purchasing: The Electronic Gateway to the Future Steven Marks	$14.95
Leasing Smart Craig A. Melby and Jane Utzman	$14.95
MRO Purchasing Peter L. Grieco, Jr.	$14.95

CONTRACT MANAGEMENT SERIES

The Complete Guide to Contracts Management For Facilities Services John P. Mahoney and Linda S. Keckler	$18.95
The Complete Guide to Contracts Management For Components John P. Mahoney and Linda S. Keckler	$23.95
The Complete Guide to Contracts Management For Promotional Services William F. Badenhoff and John P. Mahoney	$18.95
The Complete Guide to Contracts Management For Business Practices William F. Badenhoff and John P. Mahoney	$23.95
The Complete Guide to Contracts Management For Office Services John P. Mahoney and William F. Badenhoff	$16.95
The Complete Guide to Contracts Management For Peripherals John P. Mahoney and William F. Badenhoff	$23.95
The Complete Guide to Contracts Management For Capital Equipment John P. Mahoney and William F. Badenhoff	$14.95
The Complete Guide to Contracts Management For Human Resources Services John P. Mahoney and Linda S. Keckler	$16.95
The Complete Guide to Contracts Management For Security Services William F. Badenhoff and John P. Mahoney	$16.95
The Complete Guide to Contracts Management For Contract Manufacturing John P. Mahoney and William F. Badenhoff	$23.95

The Complete Guide to Contracts Management For Distributors John P. Mahoney and William F. Badenhoff	$18.95
The Complete Guide to Contracts Management For Transportation and Logistics Services Volume 1 John P. Mahoney and Linda S. Keckler	$18.95
The Complete Guide to Contracts Management For Transportation and Logistics Services Volume 2 John P. Mahoney and Linda S. Keckler	$18.95
The Complete Guide to Contracts Management For Travel Services John P. Mahoney and Linda S. Keckler	$16.95

PURCHASING VIDEO EDUCATION SERIES

Supplier Certification The Path to Excellence

Tape 1: Why Supplier Certification?	$395.00
Tape 2: Quality at the Supplier	$395.00
Tape 3: How to Select a Supplier	$395.00
Tape 4: Supplier Surveys and Audits	$395.00
Tape 5: Supplier Quality Agreements	$395.00
Tape 6: Supplier Ratings	$395.00
Tape 7: Phases of Supplier Certification	$395.00
Tape 8: Implementing a Supplier Cert. Program	$395.00
Tape 9: Evaluating Your Supplier Cert. Program	$395.00
Complete Nine Tape Series	$1,995.00

PURCHASING AUDIO TAPES

The World of Negotiations: How to Win Every Time $39.95

PURCHASING SOFTWARE

Supplier Survey and Audit Software $395.00
Developed by Professionals For Technology , Inc.

ContractWare™
    Developed by The Leadership Companies, Inc.

Business Practices	$599.00
Capital Equipment	$599.00
Components	$599.00
Peripherals	$599.00
Contract Manufacturing	$599.00
Distributors	$599.00
Facilities Management	$599.00
Human Resources	$599.00
Office Services	$599.00
Promotional Services	$599.00
Security Services	$599.00
Transportation and Logistics	$599.00
Travel Services	$599.00

Site License (unlimited users per site)	Call
Corporate License (unlimited users, unlimited sites)	Call
Administrative Library Database (requires site of corporate license)	Call

CyberBase™
    Client Server Software containing all 14 contract families
    Developed by the Leadership Companies, Inc.

Individual Server Licenses	Call
Corporate License (unlimited servers, unlimited users)	Call
Additional Installations	Call

ADDITIONAL PROFESSIONAL TEXTBOOKS

Failure Modes and Effects Analysis: Predicting and Preventing Problems Before They Occur Paul Palady	$39.95

Made In America: The Total Business Concept $29.95
    Peter L. Grieco, Jr. and Michael W. Gozzo
Reengineering Through Cycle Time Management $39.95
    Wayne L. Douchkoff and Thomas E. Petroski
Behind Bars: Bar Coding Principles and Applications $39.95
    Peter L. Grieco, Jr., Michael W. Gozzo and C.J. Long
People Empowerment: Achieving Success from Involvement $39.95
    Michael W. Gozzo and Wayne L. Douchkoff
Activity Based Costing: The Key to World Class Performance $18.00
    Peter L. Grieco, Jr. and Mel Pilachowski